W9-ALK-596

BRIGHT
IDEA
BOOKS

ZOMBIES

by Bradley Cole

CAPSTONE PRESS
a capstone imprint

Bright Idea Books are published by Capstone Press
1710 Roe Crest Drive, North Mankato, Minnesota 56003
www.mycapstone.com

Library of Congress Cataloging-in-Publication Data
Names: Cole, Bradley, author.
Title: Zombies / by Bradley Cole.
Description: North Mankato, MN : Capstone Press, 2020. | Series: Monster
    histories | Includes index.
Identifiers: LCCN 2018060991 (print) | LCCN 2019008824 (ebook) | ISBN
    9781543571424 (ebook) | ISBN 9781543571288 (hardcover) | ISBN
    9781543575057 (pbk.)
Subjects: LCSH: Zombies--Juvenile literature.
Classification: LCC GR830.Z65 (ebook) | LCC GR830.Z65 C65 2020 (print) | DDC 398.21--dc23
LC record available at https://lccn.loc.gov/2018060991

All internet sites appearing in back matter were available and accurate when this book was sent
to press.

Editorial Credits
Editor: Claire Vanden Branden
Designer: Becky Daum
Production Specialist: Colleen McLaren

Photo Credits
Alamy: Mireille Vautier, 8–9; iStockphoto: leolintang, cover, Lorado, 17, milosducati, 25, vicnt,
14–15; Newscom: CSU Archives/Everett Collection, 6; Shutterstock Images: Deborah Kolb, 20–21,
Esteban Die Ros, 5, Kiselev Andrey Valerevich, 26–27, leolintang, 18–19, leolintang, 30–31, Maxal
Tamor, 12–13, Sergey Shubin, 11, 28, YuliyaOchkan, 23

Design Elements: Shutterstock Images, Red Line Editorial

Printed in the United States of America.
PA70

TABLE OF CONTENTS

CHAPTER 1

THE
Undead

Something slowly walks down the street. It holds its arms out. Its skin is gray. It is a zombie. It is **undead**. The zombie is hungry. It wants to eat people's brains. But no one is near. It keeps walking.

Zombies often make low moans and groans when they walk.

5

Enslaved people in Haiti were forced to work in the sugarcane fields for little or no pay.

6

Zombies are in many television shows and movies. They are also in books and video games. But tales of zombies came long before any of these.

The stories began in the 1600s. Europeans took people from Africa. They brought them to Haiti. The Europeans enslaved the people.

The slaves were treated horribly. Many died. They were afraid. Some people in Haiti practiced **voodoo**. They said they could bring the dead back to life. Then the Africans would be slaves forever. They made some slaves take a **poison**. It caused them to lose control of their bodies. They had no **will**. People told the slaves it was magic. Many believed it was real. Over time this turned into the story of the zombie.

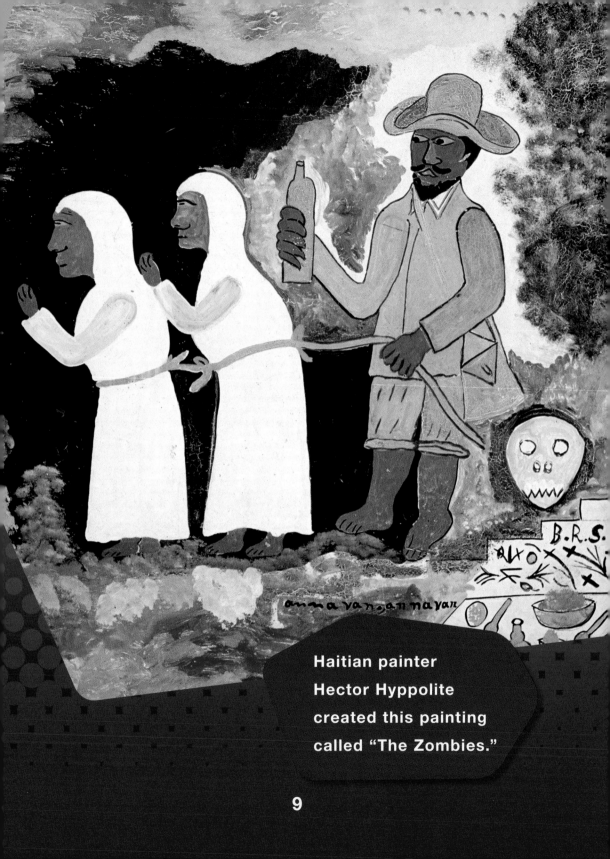

Haitian painter Hector Hyppolite created this painting called "The Zombies."

CHAPTER 2

A NEW
World

Many years later movies told zombie stories. These zombies also had no will. They came back from the dead too. But these zombies only wanted one thing. They wanted to feast on brains.

EARLY MOVIES

Early movies did not use the name zombie. They used "ghoul" instead.

Most zombies cannot think for themselves. They can only focus on finding human brains.

In most zombie stories the biohazard symbol is used to mean there is danger nearby.

STORIES TODAY

Today many zombie stories start with a sickness. One person gets sick. That person dies. Then the person comes back as a zombie. The zombie bites other people. The sickness is passed on.

Soon there are many zombies. They take over the earth. A new world begins. Only the strongest and smartest survive.

ANIMAL ZOMBIES

Some stories even have animals as zombies. Animal zombies eat brains too.

In many zombie stories the world is full of destruction.

CHAPTER 3

WHAT ARE Zombies Like?

Zombies always look dead. They are often covered in blood. Sometimes their eyes glow. Some zombies are green. But most are gray. Zombies are often missing body parts. Some are missing parts of an arm or a leg.

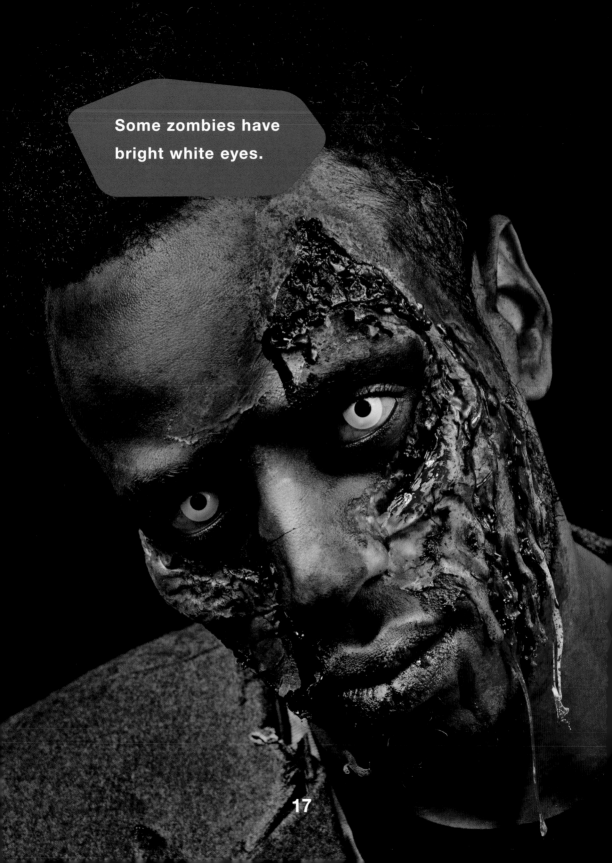

Some zombies have bright white eyes.

ON THE HUNT

Zombies are almost always on the hunt. They need brains to eat. They often move very slowly. But some stories show zombies as really fast. They can be faster than people.

In most stories zombies cannot see. They find people by smelling or hearing them.

Zombies often travel in groups.

HOW TO KILL A ZOMBIE

Zombies could live forever. In most stories there is only one way to kill a zombie. That is by hitting or shooting it in the head.

In most stories zombies are hard to kill.

21

CHAPTER 4

ZOMBIES
Today

Zombie stories started long ago. Now these stories are popular all over the world.

People like to watch zombie movies and television shows. Many kids like playing zombie video games. In these games they run from zombies. They also try to kill as many zombies as they can.

Some zombie video games include building walls or barriers to keep the zombies out.

Many people also dress up as zombies for Halloween. Some are zombie doctors or cheerleaders. Others are zombie football players or dolls. Any costume can be made into a zombie.

Some people dress up as zombie police officers.

Zombie stories are exciting and scary.

More and more zombie stories are being told today. Most stories are scary. Some people enjoy being afraid. They think about what would happen if zombies were real. They think about how they would survive. Zombie stories will continue to interest people for many years.

GLOSSARY

poison
something that can harm or kill someone

undead
the state of being dead but still able to move and sometimes even talk

voodoo
a religion that started in Africa and is mostly practiced in Haiti

will
the power to choose or control what you do

TRIVIA

1. Some people believe the ancient Greeks were the first people to come up with the zombie story. Scientists discovered bodies in ancient graves that were weighed down by stones and rocks. This may have been to prevent the bodies from rising from the dead.

2. In 2011 the United States government created a plan in case zombies were to really attack people. The plan was a joke. It was made to train government employees. It was a fun way for government workers to learn how to prepare for real worldwide emergencies. The plan included training the public on zombie awareness and steps to follow after the zombie threat was over.

ACTIVITY

MAKE A SURVIVAL PLAN

Imagine you are in a zombie movie. You need to make a plan in order to survive. What is the first thing you try to find? Do you go for medical supplies, or do you find food first? Will you hide, or will you risk being seen by a zombie to find other survivors? Tell your plan to a friend.

FURTHER RESOURCES

Want to learn more about surviving in a zombie world? Check out these resources:

National Geographic Kids: 7 Steps to Surviving an Apocalypse (According to Science!)
https://www.natgeokids.com/uk/discover/science/general-science/zombie-apocalypse-survival

Wacholtz, Anthony. *Can You Survive a Zombie Apocalypse?* You Choose: Doomsday. North Mankato, Minn.: Capstone Press, 2016.

Interested in reading about other undead monsters? Learn more with this resource:

Gale, Ryan. *Vampires*. Monster Histories. North Mankato, Minn.: Capstone Press, 2020.

INDEX